Granny's Tails

Next Door to Heaven

True stories behind the scenes in a veterinary hospital

Pam Bell

EnerPower Press
P.O. Box 841
Gonzalez, FL 32560
enerpowerpress.com
October, 2012

Cover Design: Henry E. Neufeld

ISBN10: 1-938434-07-2
ISBN13: 978-1-938434-07-5
Library of Congress Control Number: 2012949737

EnerPower Press
P. O. Box 841
Gonzalez, FL 32560

enerpowerpress.com

(EnerPower Press is an imprint of Energion Publications)

Table of Contents

Foreword

All things bright and beautiful,
All creatures great and small,
All things wise and wonderful:
The Lord God made them all. – Cecil F. Alexander (1848)

It's a wonderful privilege to work with animals and people who care for them. For many years Pam Bell has worked with me at Pine Forest Animal Clinic, where the stories in this little collection are set. The stories reflect the variety of experiences involved in a veterinary practice.

Pam has also been giving her time to the Hotel for Dogs and Cats, which will benefit from the sales of this book. My staff and I have been privileged to help launch and support this facility.

I pray that you will enjoy these stories and that they will encourage you to become involved in helping to care for all of God's creatures.

– David Perrett, DVM

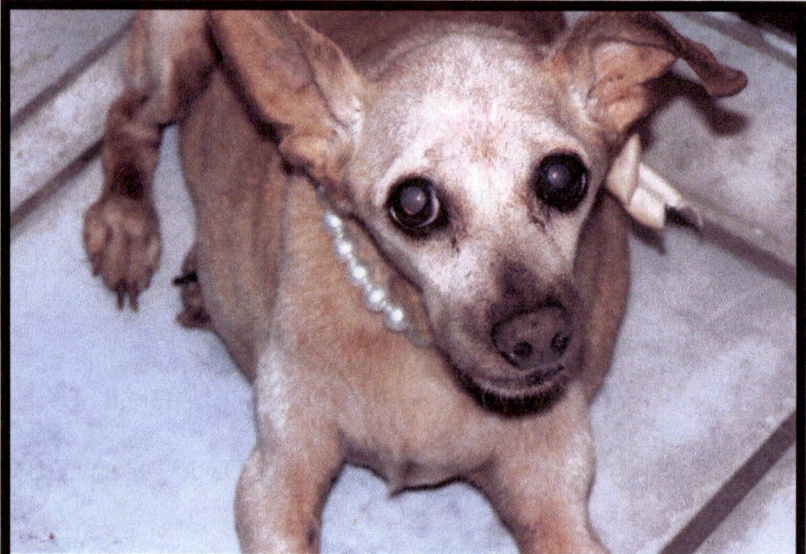

Moving in next door to heaven.

Granny

Monday morning, 9:00 a.m. – a time of the week when everyone is in a hurry to start their week.

I belonged to a little sickly, elderly lady. The physical therapist came promptly to visit her Monday at 8:00 a.m. and he kindly let me outside. After his treatment on my owner, he put her back to bed and told her goodbye – anxious to get on with his schedule. He forgot that I was outside, and like my owner, I moved slowly with arthritis and pain. He quickly backed out of the driveway and I couldn't get out of the way. I lay motionless on the driveway.

The therapist realized that he had backed over me. He immediately jumped out and picked me up as I screamed in pain. Without telling anyone where we were going, we started on a fast, panicked ride to the nearest animal hospital. I knew that I might die. My back and legs hurt so much I thought of my owner, my home, and my couch and that's where I wanted to be.

He screeched the car to a stop at the front door of the animal hospital and ran in. A pretty girl in the front office took me and this big burly therapist named Steve to an exam room. A technician came right in and said that she would get the doctor right away!

I knew that I would not be alright. No dog that was as broken as I was could be okay after a car had backed over her. I only weighed 13 lbs and I was . . . OLD!

A kind veterinarian came in and listened to my heart and lungs and that was all okay, but that was the only thing that was. He tried to examine my back end but I couldn't take the pain. He looked at this man that brought me there – the one that backed over me – and said, "Her pelvis and both back legs are fractured. She will never walk again most likely." I thought about my life – jumping up on my owner's bed and couch. I loved to be in those places and now I didn't know where I was or who these people were.

The veterinarian said that he would call my owner's daughter and the big therapist said how awful he felt and that he would pay for all my medical bills to fix me up – but I didn't think that I could be fixed.

During the day I heard lot of talk about me. I was given medication for pain and put on a blanket in a warm cage. Then

1

I heard the phone call to my owner's daughter. I heard the exact words: "Put her to sleep – it's for the best. She'll never walk again."

I saw a girl bring a shot with pink medicine in it and lay it by my cage. I knew that I would die soon – without even saying goodbye to my owner. I shook with pain and fear.

The doctor called for the technician to bring me out to be euthanized. A different technician came to get me. She looked me in the eyes and said, "You will be okay." She took me to the veterinarian and said, "We can't put her to sleep. Look at her face." He looked at me in the face and said, "Okay, let's see how she does. She will probably never walk again."

The phone calls started again and my owner's daughter agreed to allow them to try to help me. She released ownership to them – whoever they were.

The therapist who ran over me never called back and never paid my bill, but I knew I was safe and … I would be okay. That girl told me I would. That shot with the put-to-sleep solution disappeared.

Over the next six weeks I missed my couch and my owner. I never talked to her again. The people at the hospital were kind. They cared for me with love and carried me around everywhere. I couldn't even go outside to go potty. I made stinky messes and they cleaned them up. I whimpered from pain and they gave me medicine. I couldn't reach my dishes to eat or drink and they moved them for me. I felt like a helpless dog.

Then one day I tried my hardest to stand. Then I stumbled and walked down the hall. It hurt but I did it!! Everyone started yelling – "She's walking!" Everyone was so excited – mostly me! I could finally go home, the place I missed so much.

So the phone calls started again to my owner's daughter. "She's walking! Come take her home." And then I realized they didn't want me any more. My owner was in a nursing home. Her daughter didn't want to deal with me. I was homeless and so sad. The therapist that ran me over never even called back. I listened and found out that I would live at the hospital with my new name – Granny.

I adjusted quickly to my new home. Many people loved me. The people that brought their pets there grew to know me and always ask where I was. Being off that couch actually felt good.

I became a busybody. I saw everything that happens in an animal hospital. Sadness, happiness, life, death, and miracles. This is my story and my life and I'm going to tell you all the things that I have seen. I heard and saw it all – I WAS GRANNY!

Granny – Surveying her space!

Blue Boy

A small elderly lady sat in the exam room with her grandson and a very sick parakeet on the floor of its cage. She was crying quietly.

"He's very, very sick," she said.

As the doctor took him in his hands, she said, "He's 25 years old."

Not possible, thought the doctor. Parakeets only live to be six or eight years old. The doctor took him out into the hall to place him in the incubator. The grandson stepped out quickly and grabbed his arm. "Doctor," he said. "He's not 25 years old. This is the fifth one we've had for Grandma. We just replace it every time it dies. She doesn't know."

So the parakeet died, the grandson was notified later that day, and he made a quick trip to the pet store to make another miracle happen.

Blue Boy – Finds the fountain of youth.

Dixie – The Wrong Dog
(a lesson in forgiveness)

The surgery board – all daily surgery patients were written down, weighed, checked, and scheduled for the day.

Dixie – a 52 lb. black and white Lab mix in for a spay.

Time for Dixie's sedation. It was her first visit. The technician went to the large kennel, found her, and brought her to the doctor. He checked her over, gave her shots, and sedated her in preparation for surgery in an hour. She had been a stray picked up and adopted by a nice new family.

Her surgery went great! In fact, Dixie

Dixie – The wrong dog.

had already been spayed. After putting her under anesthesia and exploring her abdominal area inside, the doctor realized that a previous owner had already spayed her. She recovered quickly from anesthesia, woke up, and had lunch. The owner was called and told the great news that Dixie had already been spayed and would have minimal recovery from this procedure. She would be ready to go home about 3:00 PM.

Then came the crisis. At 2:00 PM the kennel staff came to the busy technician and said: "There's a big problem."

A bit annoyed, the technician went to the kennel and annoyance turned to panic. Dixie was fine and eating lunch but in

5

the next kennel was another Dixie – that looked exactly the same – that was the actual surgery patient. The wrong dog had been surgically opened up. The wrong Dixie was just boarding for a few days and now she had had major surgery! This is a crisis! Disaster! Time for someone to quit or be fired from their job.

The doctor had to be informed. Same reaction. Annoyance at having to stop his busy schedule to come to the kennel, and then panic. He was faint and white and angry beyond imagination. He had been presented the wrong dog to spay by the staff he trusted.

Dixie was fine and eating well. No one else was fine. Panic mode was in full swing! This is the type of thing that can result in legal action and worse. Everyone had bad feelings. Dixie's owner had to be called and she was on vacation for another week. The staff didn't know her. This was Dixie's second visit to the clinic to board. It was Friday. The doctor had to be the one to call her.

He tried – voice mail. Can't leave a message like that! Tried again. Same thing. Tried multiple times Saturday – no answer. The responsible technician was contemplating resigning after 20 years of work there. Finally on Sunday, Dixie's mom called the doctor back. First there was silence. Then the question: "Is she okay?" No other comment from her – more of shock and questionable reaction.

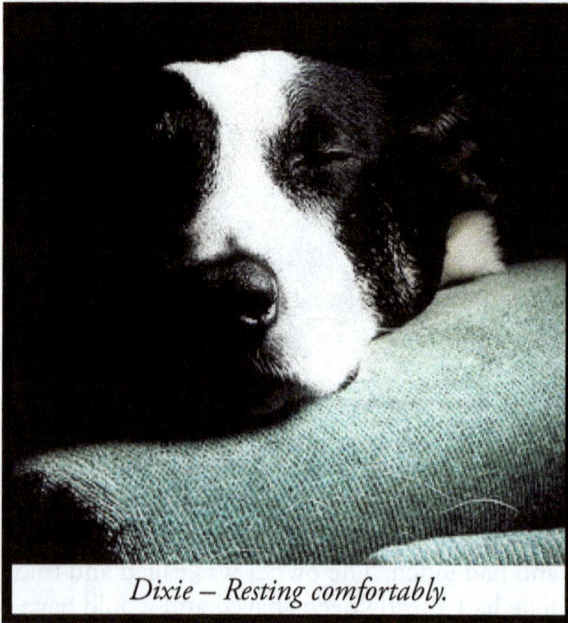

Dixie – Resting comfortably.

Dixie continued to be fine and as the week approached for her mom to come back the staff became more and more anxious. It was what seemed to be an unforgivable mistake.

6

One week after the wrong surgery took place, Dixie's mom came to get her and the receptionist put her in an exam room for the doctor to talk to her. The technician was basically in a fit of fear, avoiding the situation at all cost. At the last minute she realized that it was her responsibility, and she had to be the one to talk to the mom. She went into that room shaking inside.

"I'm sorry ... There were two Dixies that looked exactly the same ... and I'm so sorry."

Jennifer, Dixie's mom, was pretty and calm and again said, "Is she okay?" There was no sign or hint of any comment – certainly deserved – of malice.

"Can some good come from this?" she asked.

The answer was yes. Name bands had already been ordered and put on every animal as they came into the hospital for any stay. (Cage cards were already in place but with a name band each pet could be checked before any treatment was done. The owners were to apply the band – five years later this is still in place and no other error has been made.)

Jennifer hugged the technician and said that mistakes happen. Wow! The ultimate lesson in forgiveness! Not a harsh word, tone, or bad feeling.

Dixie and her new Boxer brother continue to come to the hospital on a regular basis.

Freckles

Found on the side of the road limping. A red and white Terrier mix. Had he been hit by a car?

No, unfortunately not hit by a car. Worse. About two years old with degenerative joint disease, which would only worsen and someday soon he would not be able to walk.

So the little guy named Freckles, by the clinic staff, was put on pain medicine. His fate was unknown. Difficult to adopt. Unable to give a problem like this to someone.

Freckles didn't know he had a problem. His pain medicine worked and, though he ran like a bunny with a hop in the back legs, he had a lot of life in him.

He stayed at the animal hospital for about a year. They were not sure what to do with him until the right family showed up and adopted him. They would give him a life, his medicine, and a chance.

When he showed up later for a refill of his medicine he wore a smile and a red and white sweater.

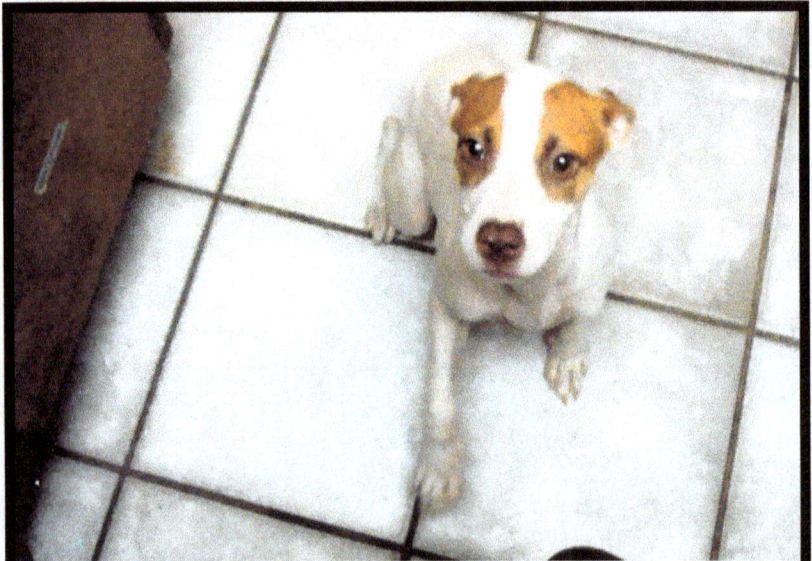

Freckles – Unaware of any problem.

Kathryn

Exam room #3, a beautiful white-faced, Golden Retriever with an 18-year-old young man named Jason – his first dog, adopted from the animal shelter. Never had a dog before and he was so proud and excited.

General check up – vaccines and worm check and heartworm check. All was okay except the heartworm check. She has heartworms. She has to be treated or she will die.

Jason was devastated. He had no money. He hadn't had a dog before. He just wanted a regular dog. He would take her back to the shelter and get a healthy dog. They would put her to sleep.

"Wait," said the technician. "I will pay you for her and you can leave her here. We will take care of her and you get another dog." Jason took the $100.00 and the clinic kept Kathryn.

That same day, the animal shelter called the hospital and said that to pay for the dog was illegal and to return the dog for euthanasia or someone would be arrested. That was a risk the technician was willing to take. The police never showed up and Kathryn began her new life.

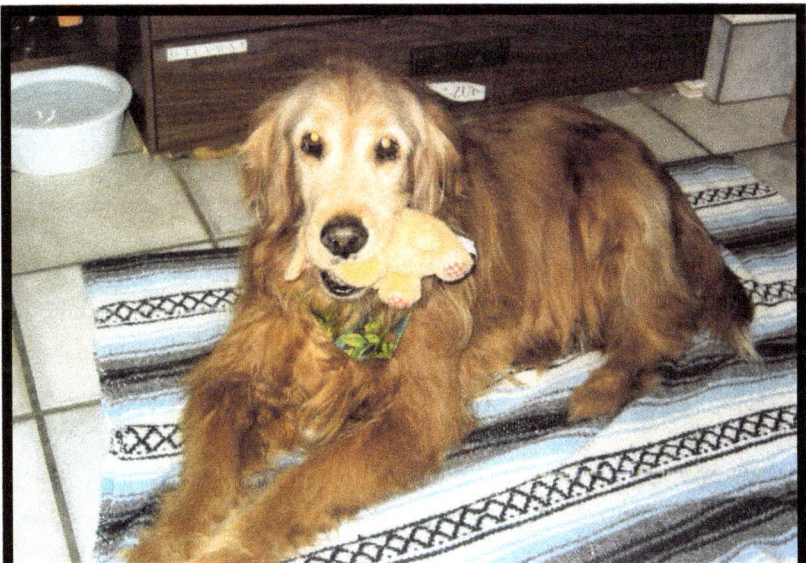

Kathryn – The day she died.

9

Kathryn was treated for heartworms successfully and went home with the technician. She returned to the hospital every day for fun and went home at night.

Only one year later, Kathryn developed a strange cough, not related to heartworms. X-Rays revealed lung cancer – untreatable.

Her last day of life she ran into the hospital and grabbed a toy as if to show that she was fine, but then she continued to gasp and cough.

She was euthanized where she was comfortable, in the animal hospital office, and her ashes sit on the shelf near where she sat every day. A beautiful life – that was too short.

Trailer Trash
(no offense to anyone living in a trailer!)

Pensacola, Florida, 2008. Hurricane Gustav was approaching and as the kennel staff at the animal clinic secured all of the pets in for the storm that night, a large Pit Bull was first noticed tied to an abandoned trailer next door. The kennel staff called the technician for help and advice – he was a big, un-neutered Pit Bull, and his intentions were uncertain. The weather was worsening and he couldn't be left out there. The technician arrived and tentatively walked over to him as the rain and wind continued. He had an old bag of dog food someone had left as consolation. It was in a lump all wet.

"Hey buddy, are you friendly?" The guy started crawling up to the technician as they continued to be cautious of each other. He got close to the technician and all was well. He walked on a leash to the clinic and hopped into a warm dry kennel with food, water, and a big comfy blanket.

The storm blew over and Trailer Trash became more and more

Trailer Trash – His owner changes his name to Razer.

handsome and nice. He got his neuter, his vaccinations, and a home with a handsome man and a pretty wife along with a seat in the front of new black, shiny truck.

Goldie

A family with three cats found a stray, gold tabby cat. They decided to adopt him. Awesome for him! He came for his check-up and blood work.

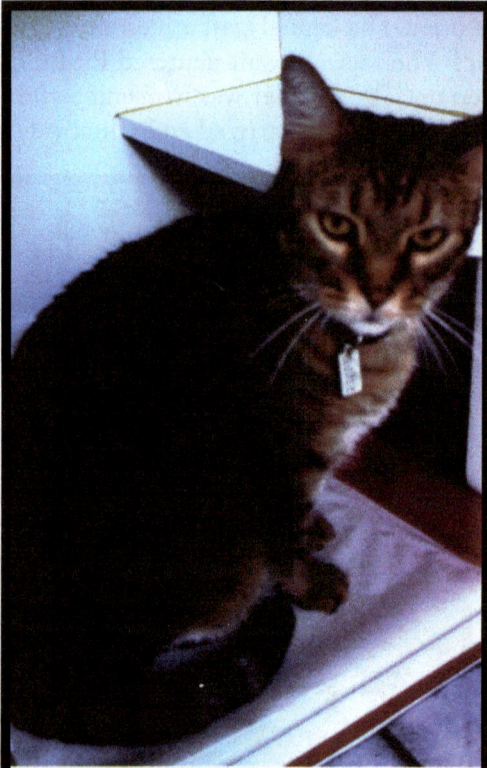

Goldie – His life changed the minute his blood work was done; although he felt fine.

Oh no! The kiss of death. He has feline AIDS. His life has ended the old way as a stray and as a member of a new family. He can't be around the other cats. He can't be around outside cats and he is left at the animal hospital. Most places would solve the problem by putting him to sleep. He would soon be forgotten.

But no. He's handsome and nice, so he stays for a year in a cage. He gets frustrated and hard to handle and begins to bite a bit. What to do for or with him?

An ad in the paper brings in a husband and wife with another AIDS cat. They visit in the exam room with Goldie as the staff hovers because someone in there is going to get bitten. And they do. There is blood and band-aids are needed! That's the end of that, everyone's sure. But ... it isn't. Goldie's going home! They understand and he gets a chance.

There's no going away picture because everyone was bleeding!

Duchess

(tying up loose ends …)

An elderly man in his 90's had been bringing in his beloved mixed-breed dog for years for every little itch, scratch, ragged nail – anything – he was there. Towards his last years he lost a lot of weight and had cancer, but continued to bring her in with the help of a caregiver.

Eventually he was put in the hospital, never to return home. He died and the clinic staff was notified. They wondered about his dog, Duchess. The doctor attended the funeral and soon got the answer about his dog.

Duchess was brought in by the two daughters to be euthanized. His beautiful beloved dog – no one in the family could accommodate her, or frankly, no one wanted to deal with her. They were trying to tie up the loose ends of his life.

But it's not that easy for the people having to perform the act of euthanasia, because they knew the man and the love he had for his dog. So Duchess lives at the hospital now with a new kind of love and life and will someday go to be with her owner when the time is right, not when the time is convenient.

Duchess – Mourns the loss of her dad and adopts a new life.

Lucy

(a hospice home for pets)

If you are a lucky person, you have a passion. Kathy Canter is a hospice nurse. When a beautiful stray, calico cat came in and was checked for feline leukemia, she was positive – a prognosis for a short life.

She seemed healthy, but veterinary medicine predicts that a cat will die within 1-2 years of the diagnosis. Kathy taught people to live while they were dying. What about a cat? Would she be willing? The answer was an enthusiastic "She's beautiful."

She fell in love with this affectionate cat immediately. She was told the details and prognosis – she didn't care. She would do it and give the kitty the new name, Lucy. Kathy gave Lucy a normal wonderful life until she became too sick to recover several years later. She was put to sleep in her arms, the true vision of hospice.

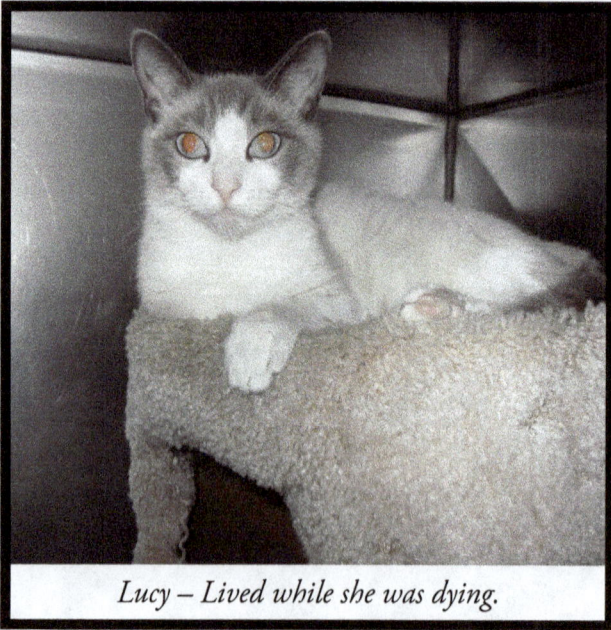

Lucy – Lived while she was dying.

Choda

Choda was a handsome, big German Shepherd found as a stray. No one looked for him. How could they not? He was well-mannered and very sweet. But he was big – very big, and sometimes, actually always, a bull in a china shop. Adoptive families would visit him, but he was 120 lbs and needed someone that thought they could handle such a large dog. Also, no one knew how he was with children or other pets in a home.

So he waited and waited. Finally a wonderful young father of two little girls visited with him. He loved German Shepherds. He loved Choda.

The staff cautioned him about Choda around his little girls and he assured everyone that he would be cautious.

Choda finally got a home. He behaved himself. He was wonderful with the little girls. He adored his owner's wife and she him.

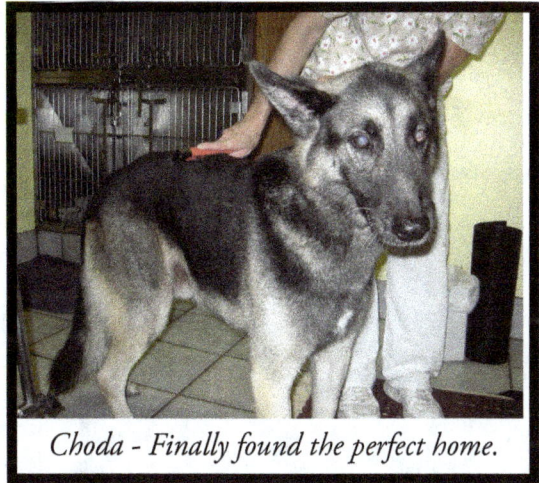

Choda - Finally found the perfect home.

And then about a month after he finally found a family he had a seizure and another one the next day even after being put on medication. The family continued to want to try to help him. Different medicine didn't help.

The seizures got worse and Choda was euthanized after he had already been in heaven at his new home.

Gage

Gage was a big, beautiful Ragdoll cat. His mom was beautiful too. She sat with worry and concern in the exam room. Her husband had died suddenly at 34 years of age of heart failure. He had been young, vibrant and healthy. Now she was on her own. Gage was sick. He had rapid breathing and coughing – all bad symptoms in a cat.

The doctor told her that Gage had to stay in the hospital for x-rays and blood work. After all was done, the diagnosis seemed daunting and dangerous – heart failure. How could this be? The same as Gage's dad!

An ultrasound was scheduled the next day. Gage's mom was frantic. She couldn't lose him the same way.

As the ultrasound veterinarian performed the test, an odd finding surfaced. The heart had another type of tissue around the area and there was an opening to allow the liver to be in the chest cavity through the hernia. Gage's mom was relieved with this diagnosis, even though it was life-threatening and required immediate surgery. At least it was something with a slim hope.

Gage – Most handsome cat, prettiest mom, luckiest cat.

Surgery was done by the skilled surgeon at the animal hospital. The ultrasound diagnosis was correct. The hernia was repaired after the liver was pulled out of the pericardial sac.

Gage recovered to 100% plus, and his mom recovered too.

Sam
(the city pig)

Ben and his mom went to visit her aunt in Chicago in the summer of 2004. They shopped in the downtown area and found an old pet store to explore. On the third floor were the pets. Dogs, cats, and a big white guinea pig. There were hamsters and fish and all of the pets were very pricey. Of course, it was a quick look and back to Florida where Ben lived.

The next summer, the trip to visit Chicago came up again and Ben's mom wanted to go to look at the pet store again. All of the pets had changed of course, except the old dirty white guinea pig. He was still there – older, bigger, and dirtier than the last year. Ben tried to pet him and got a quick bite.

"Mom," he said, "I think that we should buy him. No one will take him. He bites and he's so dirty. I'm sure I want him!"

So the mom asked the pet store owner how much he was, not that it mattered. The elderly man that owned the store said, "Take him. He's free."

Sam – A big move for a city pig.

So the city pig got fixed up with a travel carrier, a little food and a $100 plane ticket. He traveled through the airport and had to be removed from the carrier for the x-ray scanner, where he scattered cedar shavings on serious business men's laptops. Everyone asked why a guinea pig was on a plane.

The simple explanation from Ben was that he was moving to Florida.

And so he did. From the top floor of a dank Chicago pet store to a young boy's sunny bedroom in Florida.

Ben named him Sam and although he loved his new life he couldn't help but take a quick nip daily out of the hand of the boy that saved him.

17

Buster

Buster had been a patient at the animal hospital for years. Although 10 years old, he was healthy and full of life. One day his owner came home from work and he was motionless, not breathing, dead in the yard. She called the clinic and in a panic asked what to do. The receptionist told her she could bring his body in for burial or bury him at home.

Buster's mom dug a hole. It wasn't easy and not very deep, but she had never done anything like this before. It was gruesome and she was sad and alone. She had to hurry because she had to pick up kids from school. She pushed Buster into the hole and covered him as best she could.

On the way back from picking up the children she saw an astounding sight. Two doors down from her house, she thought she saw Buster walking on the road with dirt all over him. She stopped, called him, and he jumped in the front seat. She drove directly to the animal hospital, not sure if he had come back to life or she was in a dream, or what. He shook dirt all over the car.

When they arrived at the animal clinic, the doctor determined after tests that he must have had a seizure and that's why he appeared stiff and dead.

Buster's mom left him for the rest of the day so that she could recover and he could get a bath.

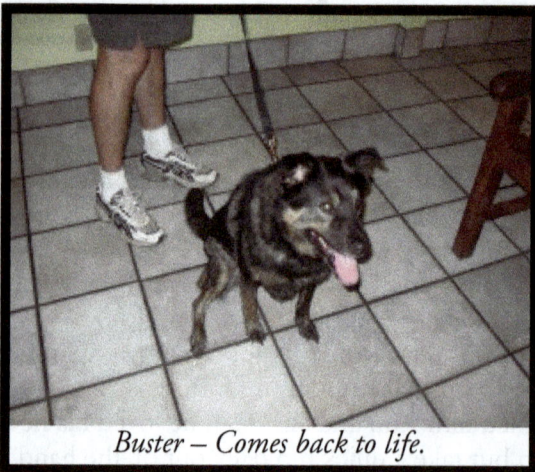

Buster – Comes back to life.

18

Walker Walker

Mr. Walker was a charming 80-year-old man. His dog of many years was equally old and had to be euthanized. The clinic staff decided to go to the animal shelter and pick out the perfect dog for Mr. Walker.

At lunch that day, two of the technicians sneaked off. They quickly picked out a Maltese mix fellow, black and white and about 20 lbs. While filling out the paperwork, trouble started to surface.

"Wait a minute," one of them commented. "is he blind? We can't give Mr. Walker a blind dog."

Well, by that point the dog was already on a leash and knew that he was out of there, so he couldn't be betrayed.

When the technicians got back to the hospital, they quickly escorted the doctor in to examine the dog; the perfect dog for Mr. Walker, or so they had thought. The dog now already named Walker Walker (1) was blind and (2) had a severe heart condition, (3) was deaf, (4) had a skin infection, and (5) promptly bit the doctor.

Walker Walker – Made it out of the animal shelter.

Okay, well, good try. Not the right dog for Mr. Walker. Walker Walker ended up being adopted by an actual child adoption counselor and led a happy life for two more years, until he died from cardiac disease.

They went back to the shelter and were a bit more careful when they picked out Mr. Walker's new dog.

Gizmo and Junior

Gizmo and Junior were two small, black dogs who were brothers. Gizmo was older and blind. They came into the animal hospital regularly for shots, check-ups, and boarding, etc.

One sad day only Junior came and the owner reported that Gizmo had died, and Junior had seen it and tried to help.

Both brothers were on long leashes outside. Somehow Gizmo got off his leash and fell into the swimming pool. The owner said that Junior was barking and barking, but she didn't know why. Finally Junior stopped, and when she went outside, Gizmo was at the bottom of the pool.

Jr. – A sad witness.

Gravy

Saturday 11:50 a.m., 10 minutes before the noon closing, a frantic phone call comes in. A dog has been found hit by a car. They are on the way – no other information, such as how big or what kind of dog, what type of injury. Is it even alive? Everyone goes on high alert and on edge, preparing emergency medications and equipment.

And in the door they come, a small brown Poodle with seizures and a frantic, pretty young girl crying. Nobody else stopped when the dog was hit, but she did, even though he was not her dog.

The procedures begin. The technician and the doctor work with the dog. The receptionist calms the lady, gets her name and

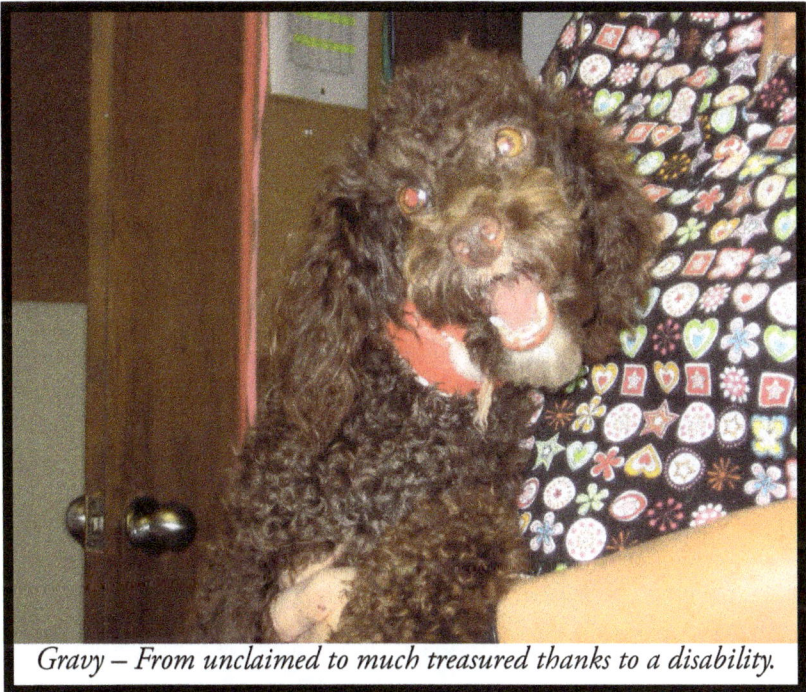

Gravy – From unclaimed to much treasured thanks to a disability.

phone number, assures her that we will take good care of the dog, and thanks her profusely for bringing him in.

The little brown dog had been hit in the head by a car. Though he continued to breathe, there were periodic seizures. He was given the emergency drugs, an I.V. catheter was in place and then it was time to wait and see if he would come out of it or die quickly due to the head trauma.

He continued to have emergency supportive care throughout the weekend. One eye was slightly open and he continued to twist to one side. When he was first given a taste of water in a syringe he licked it and swallowed. Through that one eye that was open, the technician could see that he was there and trying to get better. He never resisted any treatment and almost tried to cooperate.

The entire next week he continued to lie on his side but opened his eyes. He could not sit up or even be helped upright without becoming very agitated. Yet – he waited to be laid in the grass to go potty. He started to lick food from the staff's hands.

Weeks two and three went by with each day showing a small baby step of improvement. His previous owner never looked for him. He was lost but not missed. His name became Gravy.

One month after his accident he could walk a step or two and then fall over. He was put in the front office to begin true "rehab." The receptionists babied him and all of the clients asked about him and what had happened.

One of the clients, Laura, of whom everyone is very fond, immediately fell in love with him. She first met him with his head all tilted and stumbling around and exclaimed, "I want him!"

The staff explained he had problems and probably always would. She let them know that she would keep checking on him and, every other day, she did indeed faithfully do that.

About two months after his accident Gravy could walk with some stumbling, his head always tilted to the left. He packed his bags and went home in the front seat of a red Mercedes – his ears blowing in the wind and his head bouncing happily to the left.

Leah D. Ditch

It was pouring rain, the type of day to stay inside. A lady came to the front desk of the animal hospital and asked the receptionist, "Can you take a dog we found in the drainage ditch, about to be washed down in running water?"

"Where is she?" She was in the car with the kids, the staff learned. Of course "bring her in" was the message.

In came a very wet, matted, blind, small Shih Tzu-type dog, carried by a 10-year-old boy.

Upon examination by the doctor, she was found to be totally blind, covered with stickers and mats. The staff cleaned her up and began medicating her dry, cracking eyes.

Leah D. Ditch was found in a drainage ditch of a beautiful neighborhood and now her world consists of a warm comfy bed which she loves and people who will never allow her to be in harm's way again.

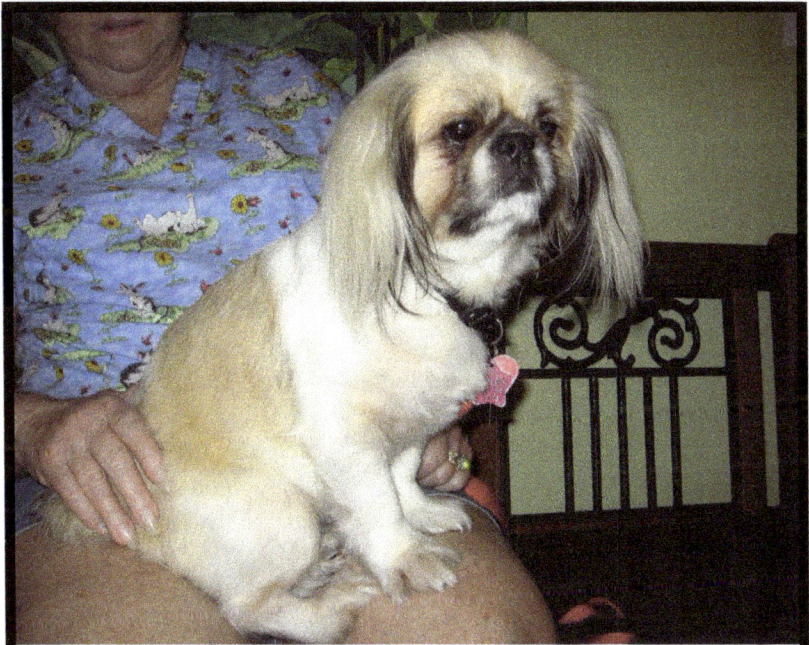

Leah D. Ditch – Leah Drainage Ditch,
but she ditched that middle name.

Lieutenant Dan

Lieutenant Dan came from the animal shelter. The staff knew that he would get a home. He was young, Lab mix, about 50 lbs and full of fun and energy. On an adoption day, a bowl of water was brought out for each dog and he tried to get into his bowl. So the staff knew he liked water.

The next month adoption day came and Lieutenant Dan had a big kiddie pool to frolic in, so he'd look charming to potential new owners.

But no one – not one person – asked about him. Dogs came and went. Multiple adoptions were done and nobody asked to see Lieutenant Dan.

Months went by and Lieutenant Dan got bigger and got neutered. He still waited in his kennel and then his wait was worth every minute.

Lieutenant Dan pranced down the hall with a prominent dentist in the area. "Where's he going?" the technician asked.

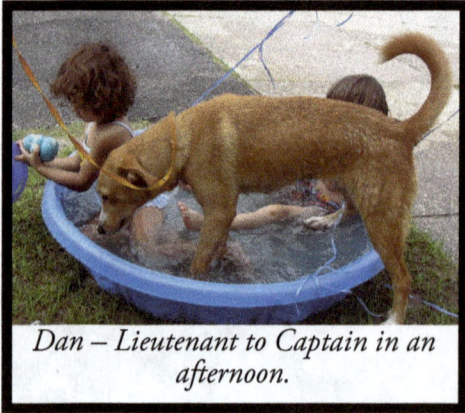

Dan – Lieutenant to Captain in an afternoon.

"Dr. Dan adopted him."

"Wait!" one of the technicians exclaimed. "He needs to take his pool."

Dr. Dan answered, "He won't need it. He has 50 acres of land with his own lake!"

"Wow! How did that happen? Did anyone tell him his name is Lieutenant Dan?"

"We did," the receptionist replied. "But the doctor already changed it to 'Captain Dan'."

Moral of the story: At an animal hospital, a dog's status can change for the better or worse in the blink of an eye and in this case, his rank changed too!

Gabby

Gabby was a beautiful, sleek, tall, long-legged young lady. She was adopted from the animal hospital when she was two- or three-years-old by a prominent attorney in the city. She went everywhere with him. All of his associates knew her and she was a popular, socialite-type dog. She was allowed in the courthouse and went to his office daily.

And then life got in the way for her. The man married a lady who didn't like dogs. She was mostly banned to live outside and under the house during terrifying thunderstorms. They had children now and she became a nobody.

Gabby – Status lost.

When Gabby was 12-years-old, the family was going away for Christmas and she was going to stay at the animal hospital. When the man called her to come out from under the house to go to the clinic, she wouldn't. He got very angry and had to go in to drag her out. He lost his temper and somehow her head was cut and bleeding. If only she had cooperated.

When Gabby and the man arrived at the animal hospital he told the receptionist the story of how uncooperative she was and what had happened. The girls knew something else was wrong. The doctor examined her and found that it wasn't that she wouldn't come out, it was that she couldn't. She had a cardiac arrhythmia and was no longer able to stand.

Emergency medicines were started on her and the man was informed. The staff suggested that she stay awhile, where a close eye would be on her and she would be inside. He was offended and said she was happier under the house.

Nothing could be done. Her heart condition worsened and he brought her back in to be euthanized which the staff readily did to give her peace in a place other than under the house.

007

What happens to a dog who has witnessed a murder? Where does he go, or what is the procedure? Actually, there isn't anything that he has to do except find a new family as was the case of 007, a Collie/Shepherd mix.

Several years ago, the police department called and asked if the animal hospital could take a dog found at a murder scene. Okay, sure. What does he need to do? Nothing!

So 007, as the staff named him, started his search for a new home. A family quickly fell in love with him – two kids and another dog. A new life, a new identify, and hopefully a forgotten past.

But when he passes by, you can't help but wonder what his handsome eyes have seen. His family was aware of the situation where he was found and never questioned or were even curious about it either.

He was a true undercover agent.

007 – Key witness.

Huey

(a bird in grief)

Huey's mom died of cancer. His dad eventually remarried. Huey continued to mourn for his mother. He tore and ripped his feathers out. His body and neck had bleeding holes.

Exam room #1 – Euthanasia.

The doctor examined Huey and spoke at length to his dad. "Leave him here. Let's see if we can make him a happy bird again."

So Huey's neck was bandaged and everyone doted on him. He mourned his situation even more. He seemed to feel that he had lost everything. He sat still on his perch.

But as time goes on people learn to adjust, and so do birds. He gathered up his wits and will and learned that he had fifteen regular people every day to love him, and he loved that. The commotion and the amazing amount of life in the clinic brought Huey back to life.

Huey – Regained his top of the world status.

28

Frosty Bite

It was a cold 28 degrees. For Pensacola, Florida it was the depth of winter. Some people said that the light rain the previous night had been snow.

The man casually walked through the door of the clinic and calmly stated: "There's something wrong with my dog."

The receptionist took the four-week-old puppy quickly from his hand and just as quickly diagnosed. "She's frozen."

Obvious questions yielded obvious answers. "How old is she?"

"Four weeks."

"Was she outside?"

"In the doghouse."

And then the expected statement: "And I don't have any money."

All of this went without saying and the small puppy had already been taken back to the doctor. She was dead – stiff as a board – frozen to death. It was obviously from ignorance or something like that, leaving a 4 week old puppy in a dog house couldn't have any other result in 20 degree weather.

The doctor again repeated, "She's dead." But he kept working on her, warming her, using CPR and all of the emergency methods.

Clients started to back up in the exam room as he continued to thaw out this puppy. This went on for 30 minutes and then right as her diagnosis of death was sure, she took a breath. Or someone thought she did. And the doctor continued to work on her. She then took another and another; she was definitely alive. By noon she was in a warm incubator squirming and crying like a normal puppy. She was drinking from a bottle.

The doctor's wife came by at 1:00 p.m. to bring him lunch and observed her, a small, nondescript brown puppy asleep in a ball.

"I'm taking her home. She's my dog . . ."

The doctor had no vote in the decision because he was so busy trying to catch up with his appointments after the little puppy had such an effect on the schedule.

Frosty Bite's name is Britney now and she lives with the doctor and his wife. Little did he know that someday that frozen puppy would be the boss of his house.

Frosty Bite – A "rags to riches" miracle.

Lazer

The elderly couple was moving out of the country. Their cat was sick and plans were to leave him with family. Before they left, they had to get him fixed up. He wasn't eating and had lost weight. He was, in general, well, sick!

The bad news was delivered after his lab work. He had feline leukemia, again well known to have a one- to two-year survival rate. They left to think about it and talk to the relatives that were going to keep him. The staff gave him the prescribed medication and IV fluids and awaited the return phone call.

As luck would have it, they called back with the decision to put him to sleep after the doctor had left for the day. The technician quickly decided to wait to euthanize him until the

Lazer – Lived a long life lounging on the porch.

morning and gave him his medicine and a good dinner. He showed no interest in food, and everyone felt bad for him that he didn't even get a proper good-bye from his family.

In the morning, the bad luck from the late phone call turned to good for he felt better. He had eaten all of his dinner, was up and purring and felt like a new guy. His medicine had kicked in. Multiple attempts to reach the family were unsuccessful as they had left for good.

So needless to say, the staff knew the owners loved him and had only made that decision out of desperation. He would have to live the rest of his life at the hospital. He grew stronger and stronger, gained weight, and was a handsome 15 lb. gray sleek cat.

And as he felt better each day he wanted out of the cage, which was not possible as he could give the disease to others. He wanted outside of the building too, for he had been an outside cat. Outside – okay. No cat comes within a mile of an animal hospital. They seem to have a sense that you don't hang around that vicinity, so he wouldn't infect anyone outside.

So Lazer lived the remainder of his life – much longer than expected – outside the hospital during the day and, the last task to check off at night for the staff was, "Did someone bring Lazer in?"

Nine years later he was put to sleep as the feline leukemia did overtake him, but not before he took advantage of all of his nine lives.

The Christmas Puppies

A daughter and her husband were visiting dad for Christmas. She brought in his dog to the animal hospital because she was fat and sickly. Diagnosis was quick – she was pregnant!

The daughter immediately called her dad, happy with the news, and then was overheard from the exam room crying as she talked on the cell phone. The technician returned to the room.

"What's the problem?"

"Dad's going to shoot her. He doesn't want puppies. But surely he'll change his mind."

They left and a cloud hung over everyone all day.

The receptionist was told to call the girl back

Christmas Puppies – A waiting list to adopt them replaced a certain death sentence.

and ask her to leave the dog at the hospital. She could have a safe place to have her puppies.

And that's exactly what happened. Molly had ten puppies on Christmas Day. All were soon spoken for with a waiting list for people wanting one.

A tragedy turned to a miracle with one phone call.

Granny Catches on Fire

My life at the animal hospital is amazing. I see so much and everyone loves me. They even buy me jewelry. I wear jackets when it's cold and my nails are always painted.

Granny Catches on Fire – "That will teach me not to wear too much jewelery."

Unfortunately my jewels became a hazard. I had on my usual beads with my name on them. I ambled down the hall, slowly as usual, mind you –

All of a sudden the technician called to the doctor in the exam room, "The laundry room smells like something's burning."

Calm, cool, and collected as he always is, he continued to look in a dog's ears and said in his mildest voice, "Turn off the light. I'll check it later."

She turned off the light and the staff on the other side of the laundry room screamed "It's Granny! She's on fire!"

Everyone came rushing over as I was stuck to the hot water heater by my necklaces. My neck was burning and my necklaces melted as I had come too close to the water heater. I was a magnet to the water heater!

The doctor calmly walked over and looked over the situation. "I guess I need to go to Lowe's and get a new hot water heater."

And I didn't wear any more jewelry until that new one arrived.

Katie

A beautiful dog, a beautiful spirit, and a true friend. Katie is a Golden Retriever/Collie mix. She was given to a technician who was previously an occupational therapist in a nursing home. Katie worked for five years every day in the nursing home. She went to work every day and enriched the elderly people's lives as she pranced around. Jumping up in bed with someone who was not feeling well or allowing therapy patients to regain balance by walking her on a leash were some of her favorite things. She knew her job and did it well.

When the therapist came to the animal hospital to work as a technician so did Katie. Katie became the willing blood donor for sick and injured animals. She helped to save hundreds of animals' lives as she routinely sat completely still as blood was taken from her neck. Being only 55 lbs she could give 200 cc of blood at a moment's notice. She did her job well.

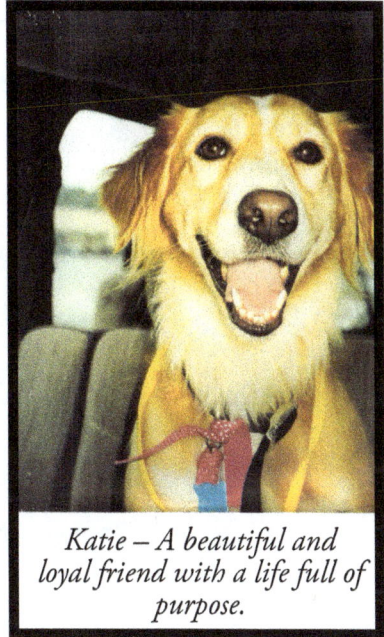

Katie – A beautiful and loyal friend with a life full of purpose.

And now she is 15 years old and arthritic and frail. Although she can't work any more, she comes to work every day, as a retired person must, to fulfill her need to be at work where she belongs.

Chicken Finger

There is truly the right home for everyone. Chicken Finger was a short, stout, muscular, white, 20 lb nice fellow. He was a "mix" in the truest sense. As a stray dog, he went into the clinic's adoption process and became very adoptable. Many people quickly loved him and then brought him back. Eight times he was adopted and brought back. That was a record for number of returns.

Most people that brought him back never explained. He was found tied to the porch, stuffed in a carrier on the porch, over the fence one day, put in the doctor's car, amongst other ways of returning him.

The only people that explained were the ones he thought would provide him the perfect home. A family of little people adopted him. He was proud. He led them out like he was the lion king. Then back they came with him after the first day. One of the technicians was exasperated with the poor dog's frequent returns and exclaimed, "Why are you bringing him back?"

Chicken Finger – Maybe my name hindered me finding the right family.

"He tripped the mother-in-law." He went on to say, "Tell you what. You keep the mother-in-law. We'll keep the dog."

Finally, adoption #9 was the charm. Chicken Finger was adopted by a police officer.

I wonder how he's doing . . .

The Twin Sisters

Adoption Day for the holidays was in full swing and the hospital was out of small dogs. The technician went to the shelter and asked the manager which dogs were on their last day or couldn't be placed for whatever reason.

She then took her on the long walk to the last run. "This small dog's owner died and she just sits and shakes. No one will look at her, and she bites!" The technician saw a cute, little, pitiful, red and white Terrier mix shaking in the cold. She immediately scooped her right up – obviously she's going with me.

"And by the way," the shelter manager said. "She has a sister. She's in the adoption runs."

The reunion of the two was amazing, a heartwarming scene beyond belief. They had been through so much and then separated for ten days.

The Twins – Mia and Little Girl on their drive away from the animal shelter minutes after they were re-united.

The two sisters sat together in the car seat that belonged to the technician's little girl all the way back to the hospital. They were so grateful and happy and well-mannered.

They are awaiting adoption together. Although people ask to take one or the other the answer is no. They will not be separated again.

Crib Death

7:10 a.m. A lady came screaming in the front door.

"My baby is dead." Not uncommon and not a good time because the doctor had not arrived yet.

The technician went running out to the parking lot with the lady to get the pet, but realized she wasn't leading her to a car. The lady headed down a road behind the hospital and to a trailer. There was a scene of chaos and panic with people and children screaming and crying.

Panic – An empty crib.

There was a stiff, motionless, dead baby on the couch.

She scooped up the baby and ran back to the hospital, screaming to the staff: "Call 911!" (The people had no phone.)

Efforts to revive the baby were of no use and when paramedics swiftly arrived they were unable to revive him. He was pronounced dead at the human hospital.

As the veterinarian arrived on the scene, emergency vehicles were leaving and it was time to begin the day. He listened to the sad account of the morning.

Ginger

Good Samaritans are around frequently. Annette was driving to work and found a small brown dog on the side of the road who had been hit by a car. She brought her into the hospital, paid to fix her fractured leg, have heartworm treatment and get all of her vaccinations. She was a truly wonderful lady.

She found a good home for her with a coworker and the picture was complete – until the next week. The husband tied Ginger in the back of the truck and she promptly fell out on the road and was dragged several hundred feet.

Back to the hospital in critical condition. Now just barely healed on the one leg, the opposite side front leg was useless from radial nerve damage and the back leg was lacerated beyond repair. So the easiest solution would be to put her to sleep, which was requested

Ginger – Always full of life.

by the new owner. It's cheaper too. Not so quick! Not going to happen!

Ginger healed in body and spirit over the next two years. She learned to walk on two legs on the same side, a very difficult feat. Remember that the back leg had also had a fracture repair to begin with. She became famous in the community and featured on news programs. She was a lesson in living life with all you have. She fell in love with a receptionist who eventually retired and it was time for Ginger to retire from the limelight where everyone marveled over her abilities, despite disabilities – constantly.

Ginger now lives in a loving home which she might never have found if she had not had the will to live her life to the fullest.

Rudy

Mrs. Greene had to leave her home and her small Shih Tzu, Rudy, to go to the hospital and then an assisted living facility. She could have Rudy there but had to be capable of taking care of him. She could not walk well, she was short of breath, and she was weak. She had lived for that little dog and she could do it again.

The assisted living facility called Mrs. Greene's doctor and asked if a therapist could work with her walking Rudy and caring for him. So for three months, every day, Mrs. Greene worked on exercises, balance, walking with a walker and using the outside door to take Rudy out. Finally, she thought she could do it.

Reluctantly, the family brought Rudy to her. They had every objection imaginable, but she was determined. She didn't complain or mourn the loss of her house, her driving, or her independence – only her dog. They were afraid that she would trip over him, or that he would have accidents, or that he would bark, and on and on.

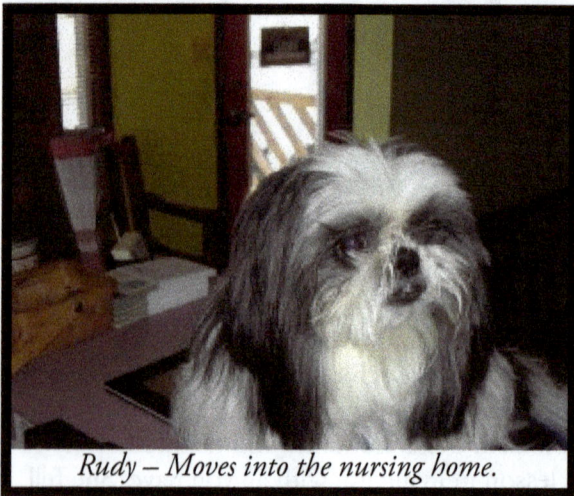
Rudy – Moves into the nursing home.

Rudy was left with her. That weekend the therapist was nervous and went to check on how Mrs. Greene and Rudy were doing. She peeked in the door. Mrs. Greene was reading a book with Rudy in her lap.

"Go home," she said. "Rudy's already been out for tonight. We're fine and you don't need to bother us. And thank you, by the way."

The thanks was not needed. The picture of them together was plenty.

Josh Dennie
(Therapy Cat)

The Therapy Department in the nursing home needed a cat to start the Pet Therapy Group. A wonderful mission – go to the animal shelter and pick a cat. There he was, obvious as he could be, a big, orange fellow staring at the door. That's the one, to be named Josh Dennie after one of the orthopedic surgeons in the community.

So Josh Dennie prowled around a large facility which had 180 patients, some residents and some there temporarily recovering from an illness or surgery. Everyone knew his name and he was often found sitting proudly on the nurse's station desk like a Lion King.

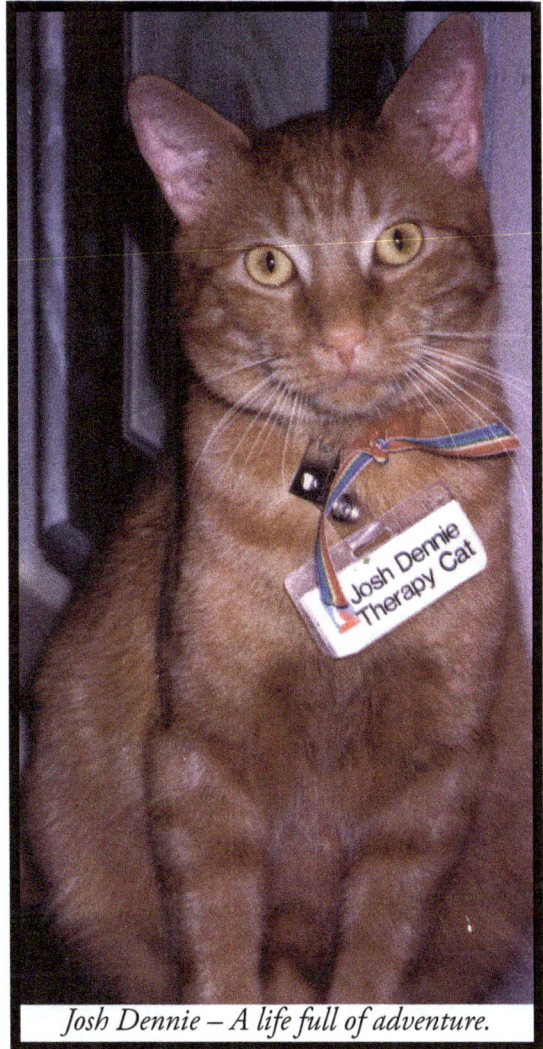

Josh Dennie – A life full of adventure.

When the therapist who supervised him left to go to another job, Josh Dennie went to her home after five years of dedicated service.

Josh Dennie enjoyed life at home without work duties but with lots of kids who loved him. Sometimes he even lounged outside in the sun just enjoying retirement.

In September 2004, Hurricane Ivan hit Pensacola with much destruction. The hurricane spared most of the house where Josh Dennie lived with only mild damage sustained, such as the garage door being blown in. As repairs were completed throughout the neighborhood all seemed well again. A new garage door was installed and the storm was over.

On a warm October afternoon, Josh Dennie was lying peacefully as the kids played. Everybody went in and the garage door closed by the automatic switch. The door crashed down on him as he lay napping and crushed his body. About 20 minutes later he was found half in and half out of the garage – lifeless.

Tears were shed and continue to be for the senseless tragedy of the lack of a sensor on the new garage door which would have saved his life.

He was taken to the animal hospital in a box for his last trip, just as he had arrived for his first check-up from the shelter.

For nine years of a purpose driven life – Josh Dennie (1994-2004).

Mr. Brownie

The Home Health Care Occupational Therapist was used to arriving at people's homes and finding many circumstances that were unusual. So at 4:30 p.m. on a Wednesday, arriving at a new patient's house and hearing loud arguing was not unusual. A neighborhood fight was breaking out and the therapist suggested that someone call 911 as she carried on the task of seeing the grandmother inside.

The grandmother couldn't walk well and the therapist questioned her about her bedroom and bathroom safety. The

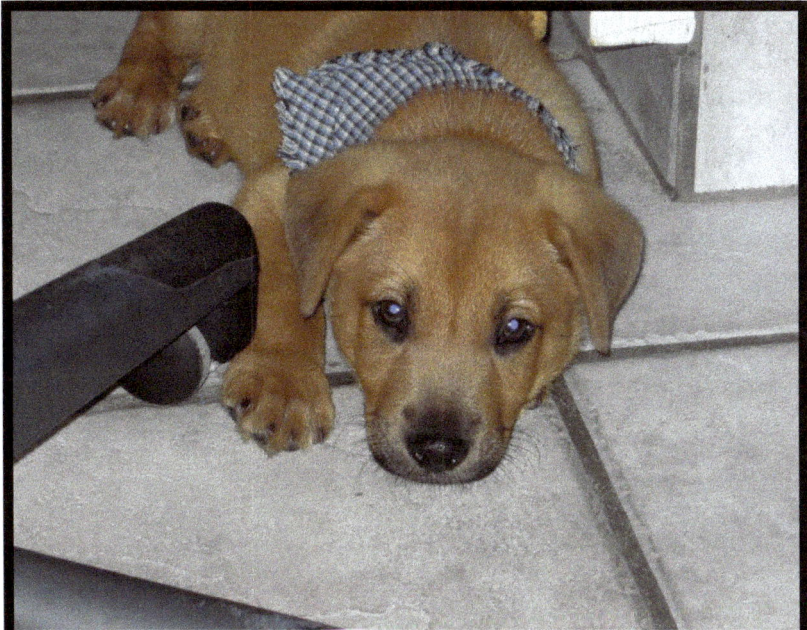

Mr. Brownie - Escaped a life of neglect.

house was not fit to live in with trash and filth everywhere. Upon inspection of the bathroom for safety questions, the therapist found the grandmother's small four-week-old puppy shaking between the shower and commode in a sea of diarrhea and urine.

The food bowl had crawling maggots and there was a cloud of flies in the bathroom. Without a second thought, the therapist scooped up the puppy and told the grandmother, "I'll take him to the animal hospital until you're better."

She agreed and the therapist planned to work with the patient the next day. As she quickly left with the shaking puppy, she walked out the front door and was greeted by the arrival of three police officers with multiple police cars in the road, which had responded to the gunshot on the porch and the 911 call.

"Ma'am," the police officer asked. "Could you go into the home and look for weapons. We don't have a warrant, but you can go in."

"Ummm . . . Tomorrow yes, but not right now, because I have to take the puppy to the vet."

Needless to say, the therapist did not return and someone else went in her place. The puppy grew big and strong and handsome and the animal hospital found him a wonderful home.

Eight weeks after the incident, the home health office instructed the therapist to return the puppy to the lady at the house. She refused and was asked to resign from the organization.

The brown puppy is thriving at his new home as Mr. Brownie.

Molly

Molly had ruptured a disk in her back. She couldn't walk. She was a Beagle who was overweight and didn't come to see the veterinarian until a few days after it started. Her family hoped that it would get better. But hope would not be the key, and her family relinquished her to the hospital to do as they saw fit.

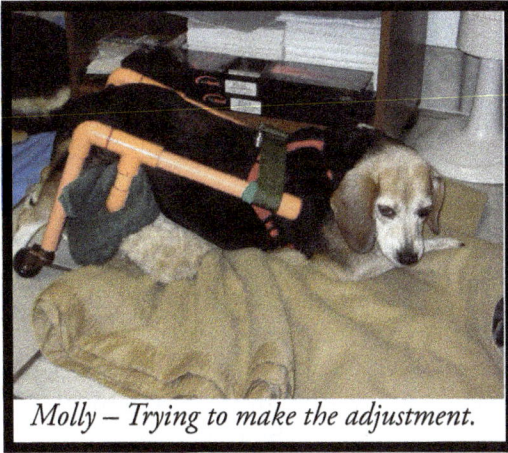

Molly – Trying to make the adjustment.

But time is of the essence and pressure on the spinal cord doesn't give time to decide what to do. Molly had her surgery – too late. She still could not walk. She was a truly lovely dog. Her face tells her stories and her eyes begged for help.

A technician built her wheels and taught her how to use them. Disability quickly turned into ability. She was in everyone's business and did not lack for adventurous days and loving care.

One day her owner came in to visit and Molly waited to tell her the stories of what all had happened since she had signed her over to the ownership of the hospital. The mom promised to come back to take her home for Christmas and she did.

Molly had a wonderful Christmas with her mom and dad, but the holiday came and went as does the spirit in some people. Molly was brought back the next week as nursing home patients return after the holidays at home.

As her face truly tells the story, more of her spirit is lost, as she sees that her family doesn't see her as good enough.

Ruby

An autoimmune disease can come along unexpectedly at any time. Sometimes in young dogs and sometimes in old ones. Ruby was seven months old, had just been spayed, and was ready and set for a wonderful life, but . . .

Ruby – A last thank you.

Exam room #3 – not eating, looks yellow, lethargic.

Diagnosis is autoimmune hemolytic anemia – a long complicated name for a disease that is just that, long and complicated. Sometimes okay and sometimes deadly.

Ruby had all the advantages of modern veterinary medicine. Her family spared no expense. She was in the hospital for a week with an IV and many medications. She started to feel better and began to eat, but her prognosis was still unknown.

Ruby went home and then came back – many times. The staff grew to love her for her attitude of love of life. No matter how sick she was or how bad she felt her tail always wagged when she was spoken to.

Ruby got worse and worse and her family always looked for a glimmer of hope, but on the day when she was so bloated and couldn't walk her dad faced the fact that she had to be put to sleep and that there was no hope. The technician who loved her would be with her as she was given the injection. As the medicine went into her vein to finally stop her agony, she looked up at the technician, licked her face, and laid down asleep on the table.

Baby Buse

A small, white Poodle lived in a perfect white house with white carpet and white furniture. She had a perfect mom and dad who loved her and a perfect small, white Poodle brother – but she was the princess.

As Baby Buse got older, problems began. First diabetes and then a serious disease called "Cushing's disease", an adrenal gland disorder with serious considerations. Both illnesses require constant daily medication and expensive monitoring. Her mom and dad did this for three or four years, which is an extreme time and requires extensive effort on their part.

But near Christmas 2003, Baby Buse, continuing to do well with her medical problems under control, decided to take control. Though she only weighed five pounds, she ate a two pound chocolate bar in one sitting. She was violently ill,

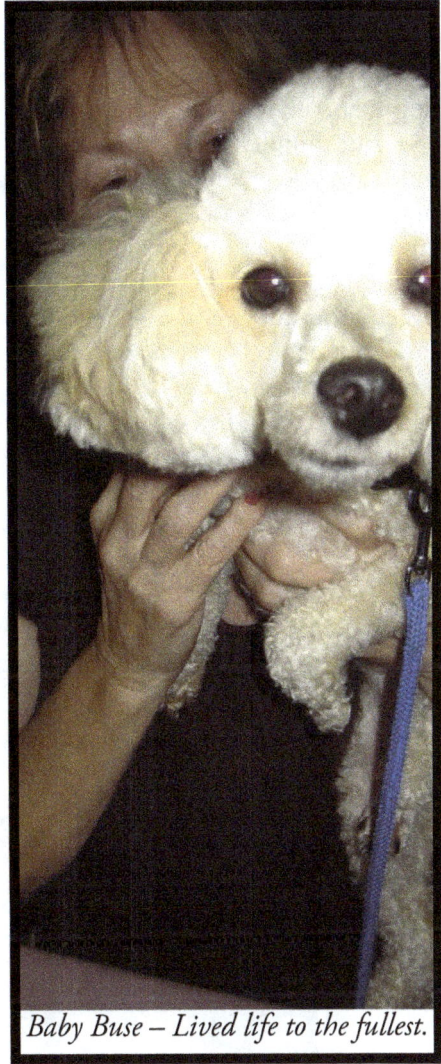

Baby Buse – Lived life to the fullest.

and although every effort was made to save her life through every extreme treatment, she died on Christmas Eve. Her family was all around her. She lived a privileged life and died in her own way, not from disease but from a big delicious candy bar.

Buckwheaties

He was the most handsome Golden Retriever – 100 pounds of regal, beautiful, fun loving dog. Never a dull moment. Never a day of ill health. Buckwheaties was 10 years old and was the type of dog that someday would just run off into the sunset.

But thunder terrified him and as soon as a storm was 25 miles away – he knew. He had to be able to go anywhere in the house that he wanted to or he would make that happen. A storm approached – a door was closed and he tore through the carpet so vigorously that he must have had 50 carpet nails in his paws. He paced around the house all day, and when the family arrived home, the blood from his paws tracked all over the carpet made it look like a murder scene.

One day a storm approached and the babysitter left Buckwheaties in the yard. He panicked and went over the fence and had a heatstroke as he tried to outrun the storm. He was found collapsed in the yard of a nursing home and taken to the animal hospital where his owner recognized him, for he was the veterinarian. He tried to save him with every skill he had, but was unsuccessful. The thunder had finally conquered him.

As everyone knew, he was a beautiful dog who would run towards, and into, the sunset.

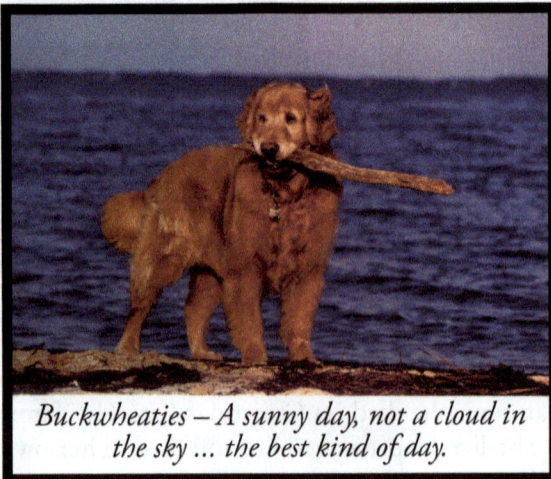

Buckwheaties – A sunny day, not a cloud in the sky ... the best kind of day.

Granny's Christmas

It's Christmas and I sit by the clubhouse in the animal hospital. It's all decorated with lights and decorations and I watch all of the sadness, happiness, life, death, and miracles that happen in a veterinary hospital.

Granny – Keeping an eye on things,
from the clubhouse porch.